PORTRAIT OF AN ATHLETE

Sinzy,

I wanted to share with you a book my father gave me after my midget year of hockey. It talks about the key ingredients to be successful on & off the ice... Most importantly having dedication & passion for the game as well as being a good person off the ice.

I also wanted to say how much I appreciate your effort & dedication to the team this year.

I know you gave it your best! I think you grew as a hockey player this year & learned what it takes to become a better one! Make sure you dedicate yourself this summer to off ice conditioning + being a better hockey player (as I know you will!)

have a good summer

Bryan ... Coach Braggs

PORTRAIT OF AN ATHLETE

Brice Durbin, Sr.

Leisure Press
Champaign, Illinois

Library of Congress Cataloging-in-Publication Data

Durbin, Brice, 1899-1983.
    Portrait of an athlete / Brice Durbin, Sr.
        p.   cm.
    ISBN 0-88011-456-8
        1. Sportsmanship.   2. Sports--Psychological aspects.   I. Title.
    GV706.3.D87   1992
    175--dc20   91-25319
                                                                                        CIP

ISBN: 0-88011-456-8

Acquisitions Editor: Brian Holding
Developmental Editor: Holly Gilly
Assistant Editor: Elizabeth Bridgett
Copyeditor: Dianna Matlosz
Proofreader: Molly Bentsen
Production Director: Ernie Noa

Typesetter and Text Layout: Sandra Meier
Text Design: Keith Blomberg
Cover Design: Jack Davis
Cover Photo: Dave Black
Illustrations: Keith Blomberg
Printer: United Graphics

Leisure Press books are available at special discounts for bulk purchase for sales promotions, premiums, fund-raising, or educational use. Special editions or book excerpts can also be created to specification. For details, contact the Special Sales Manager at Leisure Press.

Printed in the United States of America

10   9   8   7   6   5   4   3   2   1

Leisure Press
A Division of Human Kinetics Publishers, Inc.
Box 5076, Champaign, IL 61825-5076
1-800-747-4457

Canada Office:
Human Kinetics Publishers, Inc.
P.O. Box 2503, Windsor, ON N8Y 4S2
1-800-465-7301 (in Canada only)

UK Office:
Human Kinetics Publishers (UK) Ltd.
P.O. Box 18
Rawdon, Leeds LS19 6TG
England
(0532) 504211

To Verna Brown Durbin,
whose generosity and caring were unending

Contents

Foreword

W|hen young people decide to become involved in athletics they should understand that they will be doing more than just playing a game. If the game were the only thing, the ultimate goal of participation would be simply to win. As a coach at Penn State, I've tried to convey to my players that playing well, giving the best effort, and learning from mistakes often contribute more to success than a large number in the win column. I've been coaching for 41 years and I've known a lot of athletes. I've found that I'd rather be around athletes who are loyal and believe in the value of teamwork than those who think it's important to win at any cost. Winning *is* important, and achievement *is* a worthwhile goal, but participation, effort, and integrity are more important.

The characteristics that make a good person also make a good athlete. Respect, the ability to work with others, an unselfish attitude, dependability, commitment, and pure determination are frequently more important to athletic success than raw talent alone. I've seen athletes with a lot of desire go farther and become more successful than others who have more ability. Lucky is the player who has both talent and a good character!

Portrait of an Athlete contains the philosophy I believe in. Athletes who put the principles in this book to work in their lives and athletic careers will become the kind of athletes any coach—myself included—would be proud to work with.

Joe Paterno
Head Football Coach
Penn State University

Preface

This book had its beginning as a father-to-son letter written by Brice Durbin to his son Brice B. when he was a high school freshman in Burns, Kansas. Brice, Sr., acknowledged that many books had been written on technique and strategies for playing basketball. He wanted to impress upon his son the importance of attitude in achieving success in any sport. A condensation of this letter follows in the Introduction.

The original letter eventually grew into a modest paperback book published in 1945. In the last edition, published in 1979, this book was expanded to include other sports. Since the death of the author, our dad, in 1983, we have been urged at numerous times to reissue this out-of-print book, *Portrait of an Athlete*.

We especially acknowledge the encouragement of Wilbur Braithwaite, outstanding coach at Manti High School, Manti, Utah, who successfully used this book with teams he coached. A member of the National High School Sports Hall of Fame, Coach Braithwaite felt the book still has a message for the '90s. It was Coach Braithwaite, now retired, who graciously assisted us in updating and revising *Portrait* in preparation for this edition.

Our dad believed there are two aspects of sports that are important to a good athlete: a right mental attitude and the contribution this makes toward developing character.

The purpose of this book is to set forth the character traits a player must cultivate in order to develop into the best possible athlete. When acquired, these values will help that athlete to be a winner in all aspects of life.

Betty Durbin Grimwood
Brice B. Durbin
John R. Durbin

Introduction

A Father's Letter to His Son

I n 1941, Brice Durbin, Sr., wrote a letter to his son Brice B. before he tried out for a high school basketball team. In October 1942, the *Athletic Journal* published the letter and noted that it contained the philosophy every coach would like to see parents instill in their children. Today the advice contained therein remains as profound and pertinent as when it was written in 1941. Moreover, it applies equally to all sports and to daughters as well as sons.

So You Are Trying Out
for the High School Team

Dear Son,

You are going out for high school athletics, and I know you are interested in making the squad and even becoming a starter sometime during your high school career. You may be able to achieve both goals, but if you are to realize such ambitions there are several things to consider in working toward that end.

Athletics and Life

Making an athletic team encompasses much more than going to practice to learn skills and techniques. These are mechanics of the game and are essential, but you can become very proficient in sports skills and still not catch the spirit of athletics. You should not play just for the sake of playing. If that were the only purpose, I doubt much of lasting value would be gained from any sport. However, if your practice and play is built upon principles that can carry over into your life, no matter what the undertaking, then you have caught the meaning and spirit of high school sports.

Athletics and America

Ability to compete at your best demands that you develop a sound philosophy of life, including your role in a free society. You are lucky to live in a country that permits each individual the freedom to determine his or her own destiny. With this freedom comes the responsibility of contributing your part, no matter how small and insignificant it may seem, to the best interest of the nation. This tiny bit cannot be thought of lightly, because our great country is nothing more than the result of the sum total of the lives of *all* its citizens.

Your Responsibility to Your School

If you have the ability to compete, then you are doing a service to your school by trying to make the team and, if chosen, to go on and excel in the sport. Every student should do his or her best to contribute to the total school environment. Even if you fail to make the team, your unselfish attitude of trying to contribute to your school is the same attitude that is necessary in our form of government where each citizen should help advance the well-being of all.

Loyalty to Your Coach

When you try out you will develop a relationship with your coach. Be loyal to him and do nothing to make his position more difficult. He probably will do things with which you disagree. You will see his faults, but you can cure yourself of the inclination to criticize by merely looking at yourself and discovering that you likewise have many faults. Work at correcting your own faults and you won't have time to look for the flaws in others.

You are not the judge of your coach's ability. His administrators are the ones to determine that. When we come to an understanding of the things we must do in this world, we appreciate more fully the positions of others. While you are out for athletics, let the world judge you as a competitor, not as a critic of your teammates and coach.

You can help the coach by taking a proper attitude toward others trying out. This might even mean that someone else will get your place on the team. You should not expect to make the team if there are other players capable of playing a better game than you are. An undeserved victory is worse than no victory at all. Your chief concern should be that the coach be able to build the best possible unit out of the material he has.

If you make the team, whatever your position, you can be a tremendous influence for success. If a substitute, be the best possible substitute. If on the first team, respect and encourage the substitutes. Be at every practice—don't miss a single one. Remember the world wants someone on whom it can depend. If you are a regular at practice, you can be a regular at whatever you do in later life. The traits you acquire in sports will carry over into life. We carry our whole history along with us, even though we seldom recognize the fact.

Cooperation With Your Teammates

You must learn to rejoice in the success of teammates. When they do something worthwhile, commend them. Share their joys and also their sorrows. Be especially alert to the latter. Many have failed in life simply because there didn't seem to be anyone who cared. When someone has an especially bad game, lend extra encouragement. What a fine thing it would be to know that you have been responsible for a successful life simply by taking an interest in another who was about to fail. It makes a lot of difference in our lives if we know that someone is interested in us individually.

The Glamour of the Game

It is easy to be carried away by the glamour of the game and to make personal gain so important as to be selfish and only a "limelight" seeker. In doing this we neglect others and become disliked ourselves.

Never lose sight of the fact that selfishness repels friend-ships. The proof lies in your own feelings toward self-centered people. Others will feel the same way toward you, if you show selfish traits. So when tempted to sacrifice principle for temporary gain, remember that immediate gain is not to be desired. The person who steals may gain for the time being but pay a terrible price later. Life must be lived through the years. What you do at 15 will have much to do with the kind of life you are living at 50, 60, and 70. "If youth only knew what age can tell." Your face in 50 years will reflect the kind of person you are now.

Remember, glamour is here today and gone tomorrow. Let glamour be incidental; never seek it.

Attitude

Deal kindly with others. Kindness and love will carry you through when all other methods have failed. Those who tell you that you cannot deal kindly with the world and get along have never been persistent in radiating kindness and love. It is the only method that will give lasting value. Kindness and love toward others, interest in their welfare, rejoicing in their victories, weeping with them in adversity—all these contribute to a successful life.

If you never hate, are never jealous or envious of others, are never greedy or spiteful, the odds become greater that you yourself will never become a victim of hate or spite. People who are envious, jealous, and otherwise disagreeable often become victims of their own follies. Radiate love and love will come back to you. Above all, never sacrifice a principle for an immediate gain. Cling to principle always and, in the end, you will be victorious.

Of course, you will make mistakes. When you do, be the first to acknowledge them. Never alibi to the coach. Face up to life in every way. Dodging an issue does not settle it but merely postpones it. Don't weaken your individual self by worrying at night over something you could have settled the day before. When a problem arises, do something about it as quickly as possible. Give others the benefit of the doubt. It is better to go the second and third miles, for you will gain in the end.

Percentage in Life

You can't acquire too much knowledge. Study the game and try to learn all there is to know about it. Your study should be so thorough that it becomes as much a part of you as the most perfectly established habit. Read and re-read in your leisure time and meditate over it. Life is a matter of percentage. If there are 100 techniques to master for perfection and you master 90%, you will have a better chance than one who has learned only 50%. This applies to your ability to do anything. So in a sport, list all the techniques required to become a great player and practice toward their perfection. It takes patience to endure drudgery. Repetition is monotonous, but only through hardening yourself to drudgery can you hope to master fundamentals.

Respect for Officials

Your relationship to officials is important. All relationships are important, but some require more attention than others. The official is the ruler of the game. He is the final authority and what he says is law. You must recognize this and be willing to conform to his decisions. Sometimes you will think he has made a mistake. In some instances, you will know a decision is wrong. That will happen because the official is human and subject to error. It is your duty to have faith in his integrity and always believe that he is doing what he thinks is right. You must accept his decisions graciously.

The Crowd

So far as your relationship with the crowd is concerned, let that come only through your actions on and off the court. If you are a real sport and do your part, play with teammates unselfishly, pat them on the back when they make good plays, help your opponents to their feet, and apologize for any unsportsmanlike foul you commit, you will not have to worry about what the crowd thinks. The crowd recognizes real sportsmanship and loves an unselfish player.

You Are Building a Life

Finally, keep constantly in mind that you are building a life. The kind of player you are will reflect the kind of person you will be tomorrow. Live at your best in athletic competition and in all else.

You are influencing the lives of those who will come after you. Younger students are watching you, and they will emulate your actions in many ways. Don't do anything to let them down. Give them high ideals to shoot at.

Follow the precepts set forth in this letter, and long after you have folded up your suit and put it in the locker, long after you have left school and become part of everyday life in America, the ideals you exemplified on the court will be carried on. They will be transmitted to others by those who watched you perform. Your ideals will be reflected in the many lives that come after.

Sincerely,
Dad

———————————

The boy to whom this letter was addressed has served as executive director of the National Federation of State High School Associations, president of USA Basketball, and a member of the U.S. Olympic Executive Committee.

1

Chapter

Four Steps to Becoming a Real Athlete

$\boxed{\text{S}}$ uccess in athletics, like success in life, is a frame of mind. More players fail mentally than physically. Those who acquire a proper mental attitude and along with it realize that most athletes are made, not born, should have no difficulty in becoming reasonably adept at their chosen sports.

The road to development of one's best self is not easy. But it is especially difficult for those who think success can be attained by some hocus-pocus or "Ouija-board" method. If you are willing to work both physically and mentally and will give the various suggestions that follow an honest try, then you will develop your talents to a high degree and have the time of your life doing it.

ALL IN THE STATE OF MIND

If you think you're beaten, you are,
  If you think you dare not, you don't.
If you'd like to win, but think you can't,
  It's almost a cinch you won't.
If you think you'll lose, you're lost,
  For out in the world you find
Success begins with a fellow's will,
  It's all in the state of mind.

Full many a race is lost
  Ere ever a step is run;
And many a coward fails
  Ere ever his work's begun.
Think big, and your deeds will grow;
  Think small, and you'll fall behind;
Think that you can, and you will.
  It's all in the state of mind.

If you think you're outclassed, you are;
  You've got to think high to rise.
You've got to be sure of yourself before
  You can ever win a prize.
Life's battles don't always go
  To the stronger or faster man,
But soon or late the man who wins
  Is the fellow who thinks he can.

AUTHOR UNKNOWN

You must resolve to be honest with yourself and pursue your course to the very end if you hope to acquire mental attitudes that will prove beneficial in both athletics and life. The payoff in athletics goes to those who aspire to be outstanding and do not overlook any detail that contributes to success. Pay special attention to weaknesses, keep an open mind, and test especially those ideas that you are inclined to doubt. Failure is the lot of those who think they know all the answers whereas success comes to those who are inclined to listen to wise counsel.

You will become a real athlete if you busy yourself perfecting the techniques that make a great player, and you will be well on your way if you do four things.

First, Fall in Love With the Game

If you are in love with the game, you will study everything about it so you can perform at your best. Your ability to develop your best self varies with your interest in the game: little interest, little development; great interest, great accomplishment.

If you have a keen interest in your sport you will spend your spare time thinking and dreaming about it. Remember that meeting eligibility requirements is an essential part of all your thinking and dreaming. The qualities essential to excellence in the classroom carry onto the playing field and vice versa. You won't be the best possible athlete unless you are the best possible student.

Second, Help the Other Player

The importance of teamwork is obvious. A pitcher and catcher must work as one; a football team must play as a unit; an orchestra must follow the conductor. But real teamwork goes beyond the obvious. It means helping teammates improve themselves. It means appreciating what they do for you. And it means understanding the positive force that can come from the special chemistry of a team that truly works together.

Third, Be Willing to Pay the Price

Many athletes fail because they neglect to do those things that would enable them to succeed in crucial moments. You won't blame the referee for making a call against you if you spend the time necessary to perfect your game. You won't eliminate errors altogether, but you will minimize the number. A smart athlete makes the fewest mistakes.

A real athlete is willing to put in the effort to master the game. This mastery will help him or her at crucial moments in the game—he will steal the ball when the opponent tires; she will make a difficult return when the game is on the line. In sum, the athlete who has paid the price of tedious training will become the "clutch player" under pressure.

Fourth, Be a Champion

A real athlete wants to win. That's why we keep score. And a real athlete knows what winning requires: love of the game, teamwork, mastery of the fundamentals, and all that those things imply. He or she knows that to win one must also know how to handle pressure and how to come back from defeat.

But it is important to look beyond all that. First, you should set tough but realistic goals within your own sport. Second, you should develop a philosophy that includes a healthy view of athletics, of competition, and of those principles that can carry over into your life outside athletics. This means that you should have a purpose.

Having a purpose means working toward an ideal. Part of that ideal should be a concept of what it means to be a champion. The season's won-lost records can reveal at most one clear champion. But a proper concept of what it means to be a champion is not that narrow. You will have learned a valuable lesson from athletics if you learn what it takes to win and that *everyone* can be a champion.

STEPS TO BECOMING
A REAL ATHLETE

PASSION
Fall in Love with the
Game

TEAMWORK
Help the Other Player

COMMITMENT
Be Willing to Pay the Price

PURPOSE
Be a Champion

In the following chapters we'll talk more about these four steps to becoming a real athlete.

Passion:
Fall in Love With the Game

To play the game is great.
To win the game is greater.
To love the game is greatest.

F rom early childhood nearly everyone plays games. Do you remember when you broadjumped a creek, skipped a rock on water or threw at a tree, kicked a can down the sidewalk, or raced to the end of the block? Running, jumping, kicking, and throwing are nearly as instinctive to us as breathing air. Young legs and arms experience a natural high in body movement. No matter how sophisticated our later sport challenges become, this

---

The passions are the winds that fill the sails of the vessel. They sink it at times; but without them it would be impossible to make way.

Voltaire

---

basic exhilaration remains. Is it any wonder, then, what fun it can be to spike a volleyball, catch a football, kick a soccer ball, or swim the butterfly?

Going out for a sport can be fun. Just as spices and seasonings enhance the flavor of food, sports give their own distinct flavor to a competitor's life. This "high" of playing is probably the first attraction that will make you fall in love with the game.

Become a Student of the Game

Great competitors become students of the game. If you are in love with the game you will study all about it so you can perform your best. Remember that the secret of learning is interest. Superior point-guards in basketball know the game plan in minute detail and make reflexive adjustments in play. Advanced tennis players know all the stroking and tactical weaknesses and strengths of each opponent.

Your mind is capable of storing vast amounts of information to be drawn from in practice and competition, but a great mind, like a great body, must have practice. You have far more mental ability than you will ever develop but you will waste it unless it is exercised. Those who care most about the game will work hardest at developing their potential.

The mental aspects of most sports are as important to success as the physical requirements. When competitors are physically equal, the one who best understands the intricacies and rules of the game will usually prevail.

Students of the game discuss strategies and techniques with coaches and other players. They watch those who have mastered the game with an eye toward those things that can help them improve their own fundamental skills. They read books and periodicals to see how others reached the top—what motivated them, how they practiced, what odds they overcame. They think about what they have learned and, when appropriate, incorporate those ideas into their practice routine. They make sure they know the rules of the game.

It's not only fun to become knowledgeable about a sport, but that knowledge pays off later in improved performance.

Master the Fundamentals

As a result of studying the game, putting in long hours of practice, and paying attention to detail, great competitors display a smoothness in the execution of skills that often gives the illusion that they possess commanding talent.

Practice, obviously, requires work and time. Budgeting time for self-improvement through drill requires self-discipline. But the hours spent in tedious training can pay off handsomely later during the heat of competition. Automatic responses are created that are more likely to hold up under pressure than the improvisations made by more talented but less dedicated athletes. Every individual or team sport has fundamentals that can be practiced alone or with a partner on a regular basis. You are certain to improve from intelligent practice of those fundamentals.

3
Chapter

Teamwork:
Help the Other Player

'Tis not in numbers but in unity that our great strength lies.

Thomas Paine,
Common Sense

$\boxed{D}$ id this ever happen to you? (If not, did you ever see it happen to someone else?) You make a play, the crowd applauds, the players shout "way to go," your coaches clap their hands, and you have renewed enthusiasm and energy. You have succeeded! You are confident that nothing can stop you!

A great player is pleasing to the eyes of spectators because he is seen in the reflected light of teammates whom he has helped to shine.

But do you know what made your success possible? Probably a teammate's assistance.

Now multiply the enthusiasm and energy you derived from this experience by the number of players on your team and think what a terrific force you have unleashed at your opponents. Team harmony releases this irresistible force. Other things being equal, a team fired with energy and enthusiasm is unbeatable.

But that is only half the story. Anyone can be enthusiastic in success, but what about failure? Did you ever make a mistake in a close contest? How did you feel? Naturally you were disappointed, but that feeling lifted when your teammates shouted, "That's all right. Come on! Let's go!" Your coach also shouted words of encouragement. The crowd did, too. You were back in the contest with renewed energy, and you were anxious to make amends for your error. Again you have an illustration of what it means to pull together.

If you support your teammates and you always display real sportsmanship, you will have this player-coach-crowd cooperation.

Did you ever see a selfish player fail? The crowd, coach, and teammates inwardly laugh and outwardly show indifference. The player receives a salvo of boos and catcalls. The morale of the team sags. Such a team can often be defeated by a less talented team that is working together.

When Players Pull Together

You are developing a fine quality when you help your teammates improve. Bill Bradley, one of basketball's all-time stars, endeared himself to teammates at Crystal City High School in Missouri and later at Princeton University and the New York Knicks. The following was written to describe Bradley in his high school years: "It was said of Bill Bradley that his teammates were his greatest fans. He was a selfless, thinking player who could have scored more than his prodigious totals and who believed that

a foul is an adverse reflection on judgment and skill."[1] Bradley's greatest legacy to basketball was his exemplary, team-oriented play.

Lessons about team spirit can be learned from nature as well as from people like Bradley who play team sports. For example, observing a flock of geese or understanding the tactics used by a pack of wolves can teach the ideal of working together to achieve a common objective.

Have you ever been in the marshes at sundown on a day in November and watched a flock of geese winging on their journey of hundreds of miles? The lead goose's wings are the first to break the air-friction barrier, and positions are changed periodically so the heavy burden is shared. Spreading out in the streamlined V formation are progressively less strong members. Riding airlifts near the rear are the youngest and weakest, the ill or wounded.

Wolves that once roamed the western mountains hunted together in packs and defended each other. Because they fought as a unit rather than in pairs or alone, they were formidable foes.

Teammates need to protect each other like a flock of geese and fight together like a pack of wolves.

Loyalty

In a meeting before the season's opener, a coach printed these words on the chalkboard: WE win TOGETHER and WE lose TOGETHER. The coach then said, "The two words *win* and *lose* are not nearly as important as the words *we* and *together*. Our goal for the year is to fight through the battles of this season guided by the motto of the United States Marine Corps: 'Semper Fidelis,' a Latin phrase meaning 'Always Faithful.' Nothing can separate us or defeat our spirit. Jealousy will never split us apart,

---

[1]*Note.* From *Grass Roots & School Yards* (p. 54) by Nelson Campbell, ed., 1988, Lexington, MA: The Stephen Green Press.

and success will not soften us. We will rejoice and suffer together regardless of what lies ahead."

Goethe, the German poet and dramatist, said, "Talent is developed in solitude, character in the turbulence of life." Sports skills are often practiced and developed in solitude. Yet qualities such as loyalty and self-control are tested and nurtured in the pressure of competition.

Athletic competition offers a school and its community an opportunity to unite in a common cause. That unity need not be focused on just winning a competition. It can contribute toward developing good sportsmanship, esprit de corps, and respect for the rules of your school and state and national laws. Through sports you can help develop a spirit of friendship and loyalty among those with whom you live.

"Babe" Didrikson Zaharias, one of the truly great athletes in sports history, recognized the role of teammates and others in her life. She said, "Winning has always meant much to me, but winning friends has meant the most." Her credentials as an athlete are incredible. The talented Texan participated in athletic competitions over a 20-year period. She was a Texas high school all-stater in basketball and won gold medals in the 1932 Olympics for javelin and 80-meter hurdles plus a silver medal in the high jump. As a golfer, Zaharias won the American amateur title in 1946 and the British title in 1947, and then went on to win the U.S. Open in 1948, 1950, and 1954. Six times the Associated Press named her Woman Athlete of the Year. Through all this winning she maintained that "winning friends has meant the most."

The best player is the one who makes the worst player on the team good.

Bill Bradley

Keep coming back for all they've got
    and take it with a grin,
When disappointment trips you up
    or failure barks your shin;
Keep coming back—and if at last
    you lose the game of right,
Let those who whipped you know at least
    they, too, have had a fight;
When the one Great Scorer comes to write
    against your name,
He marks not that you won or lost
    but how you played the game.

GRANTLAND RICE

4

Chapter

Commitment:
Be Willing to Pay the Price

**Natural talent only determines
the limits of your athletic
potential. It's dedication and a
willingness to discipline your
life that makes you great.**

Billie Jean King,
tennis champion

T he little word *if* can be one of the saddest words in the English language. Have you ever said, "If only I had another chance, things would turn out differently."? This happens often in athletics, where success under the pressure of competition depends heavily on careful preparation. Talent alone will not ensure success in sports. In fact, many of the top high school, college, and professional players are ordinary athletes who have paid the price through a commitment to excellence.

Paying the Price for Success

Dan Gable, a wrestler whose career spanned high school, college, and the Olympics, had an overall record of 299 wins and only 6 defeats. He may well be the finest wrestler ever to grace a mat. Gable faced six opponents on the way to winning a gold medal in the 1972 Olympics and none scored against him. Upon returning from the Games Gable told a group of high school students, "I was no different when I was your age than you are right this minute. I won because I was willing to do the work necessary to win. Find your goal in life and then go get it."

Sir Edmund Hillary, British mountain climber and one of the first two men to conquer Mt. Everest, made a similar observation: "You don't have to be a fantastic sort of hero to do certain things. You can be just an ordinary chap, sufficiently motivated, to reach challenging goals."

Many sports analysts have commented that Larry Bird and Earvin "Magic" Johnson have not been endowed with great jumping ability or great speed, yet both have reached wondrous heights in basketball. Johnson and Bird are unusually hard workers. The same is true of Chris Evert in tennis. Some observers felt that Evert had far less native ability than many of her opponents. Yet by her unswerving devotion to practice routines she reached the summit of tennis stardom as a gracious, ever-to-be-remembered champion.

All of these athletes suggest a clear message: Success comes not just from inherent ability but from physical conditioning and mastery of the fundamentals.

Physical Conditioning

Unless fundamental mastery and mental alertness are built upon a base of sound conditioning, excellence of execution is difficult to achieve. Tired, weary athletes lose timing, reflexes, and even their will to win. Vince Lombardi, the renowned former Green Bay Packers coach, once said, "Fatigue makes cowards out of

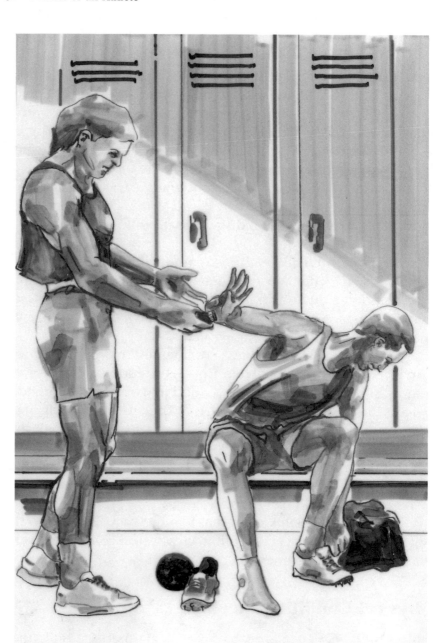

us." Conditioning cannot be achieved and maintained except through regular training. After 48 hours of nonuse, muscles start to lose tone and cardiovascular efficiency can drop off. It is also important to remember that training includes adequate sleep, nutritious food, and abstinence from those agents that are harmful to the body and mind.

Proper diet and rest are cardinal factors in training. Be aware of things that can maximize your chances to excel, and also be aware of negative forces that undermine body and spirit. Use of drugs is one such negative force.

Drugs, Athletics, and You

Team training rules, school policies, and state laws usually prohibit teenage use of drugs. In addition, every athlete should know the scientific truth about the effects of drug abuse on the human mind, body, and spirit. Merchants peddle doom and even death in the form of amphetamines, anabolic steroids, marijuana, cocaine, alcohol, and other harmful substances. These money-oriented individuals spread false claims about the performance-enhancing qualities of these drugs. For example, pushers of marijuana claim "pot" is nonaddictive, increases creativity, looseness, and coordination, and sharpens all the senses, especially eyesight. Scientifically, however, marijuana "has been proven to reduce the ability of the user to perform any function that requires concentration. Reaction time and overall coordination are also diminished by the drug."[1]

Anabolic steroids are a dangerous part of the drug scene. In an effort to grow bigger, stronger, and faster in a shorter time, some athletes have resorted to using these drugs. Ben Johnson, a world record holder in the 100-meter run, found glory at the 1988 Seoul Olympics. This glory was short-lived. Stripped of his gold medal after blood tests revealed his use of steroids, he returned to Canada a fallen hero. He originally denied use of

---

[1]*Note.* From *Drugs and the Athlete . . . a losing combination.* NCAA Publication 5570 (p. 3), April 1988.

THE OFF-SEASON EFFORT

Enlarge your sports repertoire.
Practice rope-skipping.
Develop ambidexterity.
Practice change of pace.
Study the rules of the game and read books on all
    sports.
Keep in good condition at all times.
Emphasize accuracy in everything you undertake.

the banned substance, but later made this statement when asked what he would tell young people: "I want to tell them to be honest. Don't take drugs. I know what it is like to cheat."

Of the many reasons for not mixing alcohol, steroids, crack, pot, and other drugs with athletics, Johnson has thus voiced one of the best: Be honest. Or, as Ralph Waldo Emerson expressed it, "Nothing is at last sacred, but the integrity of your own mind."

Finally, the best reason for not using drugs is to avoid ruining your life. Why gamble with your most prized possessions—your body, mind, and spirit—for the sake of peer approval, temporary highs, relief from emotional pain, or indulgence in self-pity through escape into the world of alcohol and other drugs? After all, you were born to be a winner—not a loser!

The Off-Season Effort

You are always becoming an athlete. You are not the same player today you were yesterday or will be tomorrow. You will be better or worse—a very good reason you should be careful what you do during the off-season. Here are some specific things you can do.

First: Enlarge your sports repertoire. Each sport has its own special skills but these often dovetail into other sports. For example, sliding between strokes in tennis is comparable to defensive shuffling in basketball. Spiking a volleyball requires timing similar to rebounding or catching a football. Swimming fosters great heart-lung conditioning that carries over to many sports. The discipline and concentration involved in hitting a golf ball are necessary qualities in all sports. Multisport athletes, generally speaking, develop into multidimensional competitors. Supplementing team skills with individual sports skills not only gives an athlete a welcome break from a specialized sport, but also helps develop lifetime interests and methods of extending athletic careers into other areas.

Second: Practice rope-skipping. This is an inexpensive activity that can do wonders in the development of arm-leg coordination, foot agility, body balance, and general conditioning.

Talent is a gift, but it is more than that. It is a trust which no one has a right to ignore, or worse still, abuse. Each individual, whatever the degree of talent bestowed, has a moral responsibility, not only to self, but to society, to develop that gift to its utmost degree.

Vince Lombardi

Third: Develop ambidexterity. Getting off-season practice with the nondominant hand and foot can pay rich dividends in most sports. Volleyball and football players have to move laterally left and right; baseball fielders likewise run and slide both ways; basketball dribblers are under a severe handicap unless they can use both hands. The off-season is a perfect time to learn the intricacies of foot and hand skills of all sports.

Fourth: Practice change of pace. Change of pace is basic to many sports. Varying speed and direction is crucial to sports such as soccer, basketball, football, and ice hockey. By practicing cutting skills and change of pace, an ordinary player can become a much more effective performer in many sports. A player should be able to move forward, backward, right, left, and at all angles in between, smoothly, on balance, and with deception. Most team games are built around foot skills and change of pace and direction.

Fifth: Study the rules of the game and read books on all sports. Sports have many common qualities. A knowledge of all sports will improve your ability in any particular one. Biographies of people successful in athletics or other aspects of life are especially recommended. Become a student of your particular sport and the world of sports in general.

Sixth: Keep in good condition at all times. If you aspire to be a real athlete, then you must be willing to pay the price it demands. Keeping in good physical shape in the off-season helps you to achieve peak condition in the active season.

Seventh: Emphasize accuracy in everything you undertake. Learn to do things right. Coaches like to remind athletes that "Practice makes perfect" applies only when skills are executed correctly. Otherwise, "Practice makes permanent" is a more accurate motto—practicing incorrectly can lead to a permanent disadvantage.

Discouragement: Quitting a Team

Sometimes a sense of defeat can arise because you are discouraged about your own play. Such discouragement may be caused by several things: a lack of playing time, feelings of being

unfairly treated, unhappiness with your personal progress, or a desire to have more free time for other pursuits. No matter what the reasons, the fact remains that when you tried out and made the team, you also committed yourself to work with your coach and your teammates to see the season through, giving a top effort in the process.

No coach can automatically promise players playing time or starting assignments. The coach is charged with trying to build the best team possible, and a team is a blend of many factors. Who plays at any given time depends on more than individual skill.

If you are a substitute, there are many valuable lessons to be gained in practice and games. In many cases the faithful substitute eventually gets an opportunity to compete and excel. Great personal victories are achieved by players—whether starters or substitutes—who overcome personal discouragement, find joy in the success of others, and learn compassion for those who falter along the way.

If you gain only one trait from your participation in athletics and that trait is a bulldog-like determination to see each season through, then your hours of practice and sweat will have paid off handsomely.

Still, there may be times when extenuating circumstances dictate that it is wise for a player to drop from a team. Illness, injury, changing family obligations, or other unforeseen factors may arise. Coaches and teammates should respect a player's decision at such times. And you should respect yourself if you must personally decide to quit the team.

Remember: As you go through life, there will be many reasons to quit a job, give up a relationship, or drop out of an organization. Sometimes "calling it quits" is exactly the right thing to do. If you must quit for a compelling reason, you should not view this decision as a failure. The real successes are earned through patience, unselfishness, faithfulness, and commitment to your own word and sense of honor.

A MIRROR OF LIFE

A mirror of life reflects from the strife
Of a game played on hardwood floors,
As players cavort on a varnished court
Competing for triumphant scores.
    For emotions soar high and feelings sink low
    As scoreboards continue to flash
    And the time ticks off at a relentless pace
    'Mid excitement, color, and clash.
With the two teams tied there's no place to hide
As she sets for the first foul shot.
And time has run out as she looks about—
Will team heroine be her lot?
    For emotions run high and feelings plunge low
    As you struggle toward your dreams
    Formed years long ago in the mind of a child
    Now awaken to yells and to screams.
The chant, "Let's take state!" ("We'll overcome fate.")
Reverberates in her mind's ear.
A deep breath is drawn and fear is now gone
As the fateful second looms near.
    For emotions lift high and feelings drop low
    In contests we play in our youth.
    They remain in the psyche over future years
    As we search and seek after truth.

The ball lofts in arc and floats t'ward a mark
As it spins on the line for the goal.
Crowd noise goes unheard while silent prayer words
Are formed on the lips of her soul.
>For emotions fly high and spirits dive low
>As championship games roll along.
>And gold trophies hinge on the bounce of a ball
>While cheerleaders lead out a song.
"Lord, let it fall in so teammates will win,"
Was the theme of her silent prayer.
The ball struck back-rim and failed to bounce in
Then she bowed her head with a stare.
>For emotions rise high and feelings dip low
>When you dare to try with clenched fists
>And risk your fond hopes on a basketball game
>With its sacrifice, sweat, and its twists.
A mirror of life reflects from the strife
Of a game on a field house floor
As players cavort on a flood-lit court
Fighting hard 'til the final score.
>And youth emerge strong for new battles ahead
>If they rise once more from defeat;
>For life is an ocean of ebbs and of tides
>Where despair and faith will compete.

WILBUR T. BRAITHWAITE

5

Chapter

Purpose:
Be a Champion

**Everyone is endowed with
qualities of the champion and
can succeed in spite of
handicaps in the most
important game of all —
the game of life.**

Alice Marble,
The Road to Wimbledon

Alice Marble was America's top-ranked female tennis player from 1936 through 1940. After her death in 1990, the *New York Times* quoted Jack Kramer, a member of the Tennis Hall of

Fame: "She was the lady who most changed the style of play for women. She introduced the aggressive athletic style that has led down to the female stars of today like Billie Jean King, Martina Navratilova, and Steffi Graf."

Marble wrote about her early experiences in her book *The Road to Wimbledon*. She suggested that being a champion required, among other things, competitive spirit, ability, mental and moral capacity, control of one's temper, and concentration. Then she wrote that, to her, good tennis boiled down to two things: "strict physical training and the mental discipline that makes the training possible."

Marble also knew about hardship. Her playing career was interrupted several times by illness, and her husband was killed in World War II. She knew about life as well as about tennis, and she knew what it took to be a champion, both on and off the court.

Few can reach the heights in their sport that Alice Marble reached in tennis. But everyone can be a champion at his or her own level and, more importantly, in the game of life.

Competition

To get an idea of what it means to be a champion in the best possible sense, we first need a proper understanding of competition.

Opponents should not be viewed as enemies but as friends. The word *competition* comes from two Latin roots, *com* and *petere*, meaning "to seek together." When two individuals or teams pit their skills and wits against each other, both can elevate their respective levels of performance. Winning may not be as important, overall, as the values and satisfactions gained from self-improvement.

W. Timothy Gallwey amplified this viewpoint in his book *The Inner Game of Tennis*. "True competition is identical with true cooperation. Each player tries his hardest to defeat the other, but in this use of competition it isn't the other *person* we are defeating; it is simply a matter of overcoming the obstacles

TRAITS OF A CHAMPION

The easiest way to develop into a true champion is to work industriously toward the attainment of these qualities.

A true champion . . .

. . . Has team spirit and prefers team victory to personal glory.

. . . Keeps in good physical condition at all times.

. . . Likes to see the other person succeed.

. . . Keeps in good mental condition at all times.

. . . Deals honestly with coach and teammates.

. . . Never blames anyone else for his or her own failure.

. . . Strives to master all details of the game.

. . . Knows that one failure does not mean a succession of failures, but is only percentage at work.

. . . Is gracious in defeat and thus is not tense in a tight spot (players who see defeat and victory in proper proportion are cool under fire, which is one secret of relaxation).

. . . Realizes that the difference between most players is not so great that intelligent effort cannot overcome it.

. . . Has a friendly, competitive attitude toward opponents.

. . . Loves to play for the pleasure of playing and strives to overcome weaknesses.

. . . Has a well-balanced outlook on life with sufficient interests to keep any single thing from becoming a stumbling block to success.

. . . Studies qualities of champions, past and present.

. . . Cultivates kindliness, friendliness, and unselfishness.

. . . Cultivates a charitable spirit, hence is not conceited.

. . . Knows that the sun will rise in the morning regardless of what happens today.

he presents. In true competition no person is defeated. Both players benefit by their efforts to overcome the obstacles presented by the other. Like two bulls butting their heads against one another, both grow stronger and each participates in the development of the other."

Thus we see that the final score is not the only thing that counts in competition. Understanding that, we realize that being a champion in the best possible sense also goes beyond the final score.

The Traits of a Champion

It is encouraging to note that all the qualities of a champion shown on the facing page can be acquired. When you realize that much of success depends on mental attitude, then you will be on the way to being the chief actor at that tense moment when victory hangs in the balance. This prize is bought at a price: desire of attainment, and willingness to work long hours until these qualities are part of your character.

Coming Back From Defeat

Have you ever lost an important game to a traditional rival and then observed the changes that defeat brings to the atmosphere of a locker room? Lights that glowed bright in victory now flicker and cast shadows on the floor. Voices of normally talkative teammates are silent. Defeat cuts deeply into a competitor's basic nature, leaving its own wounds and unpleasant sensations.

Yet the heart and spirit of great individuals in all walks of life have often been tempered and refined in the furnace of human emotion following what appeared at first to be failure. "Victory gives us wings while defeat gives us spurs."

The sports world is full of individuals and teams that overcame initial adversity and setbacks to accomplish unusual feats. Wilma Rudolph provides an example. As a child growing up in Tennessee, Rudolph was surrounded by poverty and

suffered chronically from illness and disease. Her physical development was so delayed that she could not walk until she was 8 years old. Yet within another 6 years, at age 14, she was setting scoring records in basketball.

What had promised to be a great career in track at Tennessee State for Rudolph turned into a series of injuries and illness. Showing indomitable courage, the graceful runner finally came into her own in the 1959 Millrose Games. There she won the 60-yard dash in a field open to both men and women sprinters. Rudolph's crowning achievement came a year later in Rome, where she became the first U.S. woman ever to capture three gold medals in the Olympic Games.

The gymnast Cathy Rigby provides another example. As a 15-year-old, Rigby competed in the 1968 Olympic Games in Mexico City, and she won a gold medal at the World Championships in 1970. However, at the same time she was reaching puberty. This brought with it an increase in weight and a resulting eating disorder from trying to control her weight. When Rigby did not win a medal at the 1972 Olympic Games in Munich, many people said she had failed. She did not fail. She has gone on to help other women fight anorexia and bulimia. And she has earned success on the stage that includes playing the role of Peter Pan on Broadway.

Defeat spurs great competitors to increased effort to practice. It can cause us to be more caring about teammates, to boast less after winning, and to strengthen our commitment to succeed. Losses help us evaluate our level of mastery of fundamentals and team play. And most importantly, defeat tests our will to practice, which reflects later in our will to win.

You, too, can come back from defeat by working to incorporate several championship qualities into your life.

First, do not place blame for a loss on anyone—not teammates, the referees, the coach, or especially yourself. No contest is ever won or lost on a single play. It only seems that way when you miss the crucial spike in a 14-13 volleyball game, or bungle the sure scoring opportunity in a 2-1 soccer loss, or double-fault on match point. A sense of fairness dictates that no single

botched play, out of hundreds of plays that could have changed the outcome, should be singled out as THE reason for defeat.

Second, be a leader and create good morale when your team loses. Banging locker doors, kicking benches or walls, and shouting laments all reveal a lack of discipline, whereas holding tempers in check shows a maturity that bodes well for future achievement. "We'll win next time" is a rallying cry coaches love to hear from teams, but better still is your spoken or silent vow to improve free-throw shooting, fielding and hitting, serving, putting, or whatever skill proved weak at a crucial moment. Great competitors anticipate a Monday practice after a Friday loss so they can improve and be ready for the next game.

Finally, overcoming defeat will be easier if you remember these words of Mark Twain: "Defeat is not the worst of failures—not to have tried is the worst of failures."

Work Toward an Ideal

As a player, you may have been reminded to "keep your head up." This should be applied beyond the court and the playing field: You should aim at lofty principles that make for noble living. After all, in the field of sports, the physical body eventually gives way and a younger generation takes over. The athletes who have high ideals receive the greatest pleasure and acclaim long after their days of athletic performance. They possess the ability to see the real values of the game, and many make their greatest contributions when they are no longer able to compete.

Some of the best positions in life await those who have demonstrated the ability to perform excellently in sports. Athletic accomplishments add experience to classroom training. The world asks for men and women who know how to work with others; who will work at a task industriously; who respect supervisors; who master assignments; who know how to win but also know how to take defeat; who are loyal to everyone including themselves; who are reliable, honest, and dependable.

There is nothing noble in being superior to some other person. The true nobility is in being superior to your previous self.

Hindu proverb

Athletic competition, rightly performed, gives you these qualities. You are not inexperienced if you are a successful athlete.

Goethe said "the whole purpose of this world seems to be to provide a physical base for growth of the spirit." Sports can be a vehicle to help you grow physically, mentally, and spiritually if you participate for the right reasons and exercise sound judgment in the process.

You will be a real athlete if you are in love with the game, help other athletes, pay the price by devoting long hours to practice, and work toward the ideal of being a champion in everything you undertake.

DO YOU WANT TO BE A CHAMPION?

Do you want to run 'til your lungs are tight?
Do you want to hustle with all your might?
Do you want your shirt soaking with sweat?
Work, my son, you'll be a Champion yet.

Can you take bad breaks in a hard-fought game?
Can you be way down and fight just the same?
Can you face the task with a jaw that's set?
Steady, my son, you'll be a Champion yet.

Is your spirit inside a burning flame?
Is your "want to" strong or feeble and lame?
Is your eye on target, a goal to be met?
Fire-up, young man, you'll be a Champion yet.

Do you feel the sting of blisters you've worn?
Do your legs grow limp from "bucking" the storm?
Do you study odds and know the best bet?
Listen, my son, you'll be a Champion yet.

Will you live like a Spartan and always train?
Will you tame your passions for self and the game?
Will you obey the rules that you have set?
Discipline, lad, you'll be a Champion yet.

Do you hear voices yell out every mistake?
Do you fear the jeers for errors you make?
Add plus with the minus to balance the net?
Patience, my son, you'll be a Champion yet.

Can you lose yourself in competitive fire?
Can you lift up your game going down to the wire?
Can you rise from defeat once the verdict is set?
Defiance, my son, you'll be a Champion yet.

It's not in the score as much as the mind.
It's not in the glory, the fame, or the kind.
It is in the motto, "You must give to get."
Hang in there, son, you'll be a Champion yet.

                                        WILBUR T. BRAITHWAITE

6

Chapter

Your Profile

T he purpose of this chapter is to help you think about the ideas in this book and make an intelligent approach toward self-improvement. You will find a checklist of 10 questions pertaining to each of the four preceding chapters. To rate yourself, answer each question according to the following scale.

5	Definitely Yes
4	Yes
3	Neutral
2	No
1	Definitely No

Read each statement carefully. In case of doubt, check a lower number; it is better to underrate than overrate yourself. Honesty is important. The intent is to help you discover where there is room for improvement as you work to grow as an athlete. You might want to rate yourself at the beginning and again at the end of the season and compare your scores.

A response of 5 to every statement is unlikely. For example, you may work hard in practice but harder still in a game. In that case, a 4 is the better choice for the first statement under Commitment.

Also, you may have good reasons for not assigning a high number to a statement. For instance, if you have important interests or pressures outside athletics, then it might not be appropriate to aim for a 5 on every statement in the first section. Of course, in this case you should have correspondingly lower expectations for your athletic achievement. It is up to you to set your own priorities and goals.

Many of the statements here apply outside athletics as well. For example, how would you stack up if you scored yourself for academics instead of athletics?

The main point is to think about each statement and ask yourself how it applies to you. If you want to improve as an athlete, this should help you find places to start.

PASSION:
FALL IN LOVE WITH THE GAME

_____ 1. Do I play the sport because *I* want to?

_____ 2. Do I look forward to practice?

_____ 3. Do I try to learn all there is to know about the game?

_____ 4. Do I think about the game and how to improve even when I am not practicing or playing?

_____ 5. Do I read about successful people in athletics and other fields to learn things that could help me succeed?

_____ 6. Do I realize that success in athletics requires more than skills and technique?

_____ 7. Do I believe that defeat, handled properly, can make me a better competitor?

_____ 8. Do I understand percentages and know that one failure does not mean a succession of failures?

_____ 9. Do I sincerely desire to become a better athlete?

_____ 10. Do I believe that interest is one of the keys to success?

_____ TOTAL

TEAMWORK:
HELP THE OTHER PLAYER

_____ 1. Do I always acknowledge the help I receive from teammates?

_____ 2. Do I always encourage players who have difficulties?

_____ 3. Do I concentrate on improving myself and avoid looking for flaws in my teammates and coach?

_____ 4. Do I want to be judged by my accomplishments rather than by special favor?

_____ 5. Do I prefer team victory to personal glory?

_____ 6. Do I recognize that jealousy can jeopardize my team's success?

_____ 7. Do I accept my coach's team selections without question?

_____ 8. Do I commend the good play of others?

_____ 9. Do I believe that I can contribute to school and community spirit by the attitude I show as a team member?

_____ 10. Do I readily admit my mistakes?

_____ TOTAL

COMMITMENT:
BE WILLING TO PAY THE PRICE

_____ 1. Do I work as hard in practice as in a game?

_____ 2. Do I have a definite plan for things I want to improve each time I practice?

_____ 3. Do I try to stay in good physical condition during both the season and off-season?

_____ 4. Do I engage in other sports during the off-season?

_____ 5. Do I avoid harmful substances such as tobacco, alcohol, anabolic steroids, and other drugs?

_____ 6. When faced with a problem, do I go to work immediately to find a solution?

_____ 7. Do I practice with perseverance to overcome the weak points in my game?

_____ 8. Do I emphasize accuracy in everything I undertake?

_____ 9. Do I believe that talent alone will not ensure success in sports?

_____ 10. Do I believe that I have a responsibility to develop my talent to its utmost degree?

_____ TOTAL

PURPOSE:
BE A CHAMPION

_____   1. Do I set goals and then work from a plan to try to achieve them?

_____   2. Do I believe that sports can develop traits that will help me succeed in other pursuits?

_____   3. Do I have a well-balanced outlook on life with sufficient interests to allow me to keep victories and defeats in perspective?

_____   4. Do I view myself as a role model for younger persons?

_____   5. Do I believe that nearly every successful person has overcome hardships?

_____   6. Do I view the opponent as a friend, as someone with whom I share a common interest and who can spur me on to improvement?

_____   7. Do I show respect for game officials?

_____   8. Am I gracious in both victory and defeat?

_____   9. Do I like to see others succeed?

_____   10. Do I believe that intelligently directed work will lead to success?

_____   TOTAL

Epilogue

M ost athletes who fail do so because they don't know where they are going. They are like Don Quixote, who got on his horse and rode off in all directions. They do not make an intelligent approach to athletic accomplishment. They have no sense of direction. They know they are on the way but don't know when they will arrive or what they will do when they get there. This is a deplorable situation, especially because systematic training would mean the difference between success and failure.

You should decide what you are going to do and then make a list of things you should do to reach that goal. Make a checklist and check off each item as you master it. This is a simple technique, but it works. Simplicity is the great secret of successful living. Many people make life too difficult. The attainment of success comes through intelligent application to the task you want to accomplish.

Success comes to those persons who (1) know where they are going, (2) determine what should be done to move in that direction, (3) work industriously toward mastery of all details, and (4) believe in themselves and in their goals.

Your future will be determined by you. You can read all the books you like, do all the wishful thinking you like, but success will never come until you decide to be up and doing. Herein lies the secret of success.

Good luck as you work to realize your athletic dreams and create a special, living version of your own *Portrait of an Athlete*!

About the Author

B rice Durbin, Sr., was born in Chamois, Missouri, on the Missouri River, on March 12, 1899. He was the youngest of seven children.

His father was buried on Brice's 15th birthday. To finish high school Brice moved to live with a sister in St. Louis, where he attended McKinley High School during the day and worked in the evening.

He graduated from the School of Business and Public Administration, University of Missouri at Columbia, in 1922. Returning to college during the Great Depression, he earned a master's degree in education in 1936.

In 1923 Brice married Verna Brown, a native of Elk City, Kansas. Most of Brice's career was spent in Kansas, where he was a highly successful teacher, counselor, coach, administrator, author, and public speaker. For 4 years after World War II he worked closely with hundreds of returning veterans who were in college under the G.I. Bill. He finished his public school career in Columbus, Kansas, where he retired in the 1960s. He then began a new job, this time with students in work-study programs sponsored by the Neighborhood Youth Corps.

Brice had a profound respect for the unlimited potential of young people and for the power of both the spoken and written word. The most distinguishing feature of his career was his unusual talent for acting on and expounding the philosophy in this book.

Brice Durbin, Sr., died December 11, 1983.